Try not to bite his head off

A Cornered Collection by Mike Baldwin

For Madeline
(Mom)

www.cornered.com
Contact us at: urcornered@gmail.com

A daily newspaper and Web comic
distributed by
Universal Uclick
1130 Walnut Street
Kansas City, MO 64106

Other Cornered Books

Don't Try Anything Funny
First Book of Cornered
Order online at:
www.cafepress.com/cp/prod.aspx?p=cornered.15195650

I think he blames himself. And me.
Business Cartoons Vol. 1

Mostly I fight for market share
Business Cartoons Vol. 2

One day, this will all be your fault
Business Cartoons Vol. 3

Are you Seeing Someone Else?
Dating Cartoons

Group Discount Therapy
A pile of Mental Health Cartoons

Reigning Cats and Dogs
Pet Cartoons
Order online at:
http://www.lulu.com/cornered

"The fourth quarter was no walk in the park. Especially for those who count on us to walk in the park."

"Nice work, kid. Looks like you might be ready to sit up at the big boys' table."

Mob eulogies: short and to the point.

"It's a private school. Can't say which one – it's private."

"Well, no, I haven't said I do yet. How quick can you get down here?"

"I still have trouble sleeping. I thought when I died I could rest in peace."

"He's not here. If you're lost without him, you can always stay and see if he tries to find you."

"You need to be more persistent. Now, get out of my office and keep coming back until you've worn me down."

"I won't be logging in today. I forgot my password."

"It's important to believe in yourself –
even when the jury doesn't."

"When I said you could pick me up at
8, I just assumed you owned a car."

"Just tell me. You don't need to drag
that out every time I ask how I look."

"Might be depression. Your tongue is
depressed."

"The chef apparently doesn't know how to accept a compliment."

"If you're still alive this time next week, you'll be living beyond your means."

DIY IT software

Help for the passive-aggressive.

"It's up for adoption. Just pay to have it fixed."

Stupid obscene phone callers.

It's hard not to be bitter the second time around.

"DON'T TOUCH – IT'S STILL WET!"

"I can't believe you'd accuse us of age discrimination. At your age, you ought to know better."

"See? You missed one. When you pull the plug, be sure to pull them all."

"You're qualified. I'm just a little put-off by your hattitude."

"All our vehicles come with a 24-hour, round-the-block guarantee."

"Don't worry, I didn't tell them anything they didn't already suspect."

"You have to sign it promising never to discuss sex, politics or religion."

"Good. Now, who else wants in?"

"Don't know where to invest what's left of your portfolio. I'd flip a coin, but the way it's going, I'd lose the coin."

"There's lots of text messaging in this job. I need someone who can just sit back and twiddle their thumbs all day."

"Looks like you've lost your stomach for risk."

"Sorry it's taking so long to load. I'm still on dial-up."

Baby's first thought

"And promise to love each other through constant drama, bad judgment, poor choices and self-delusion?"

"I thought being married to a rodeo clown would be more fun."

"Let's hold off making a decision until we have even more information we don't really need."

"I'll stop using finger quotes if you (control freak) let me use hand brackets."

"In exchange for my testimony, they gave me a whole new identity – 00761."

"You're never too young to start plan… For crying out loud, quit drooling all over everything!"

"Your table will be ready shortly."

"Yeah, I think we have a future together. Why else would I write you a post-dated check for my half of the dinner?"

"Hope you like it. I put a LOT of thought into it."

"That's odd. Your monitor looks the same size as mine from here. It looks way bigger from my desk."

"If it pleases the court, my client would like a second opinion."

"We can't keep living in the fast-food lane."

"It's easy. As my old English teacher used to say, just write what you know."

"Tonight's special is out of this world. Have your passports ready."

"No, I'm not going to go back to ask for a little more wiggle room."

"Duly noted. Now, shall we move on or does anyone else feel the need to have a conniption?"

"Nowadays, I spend a lot of time making amends. I have no idea why. There's no market for them."

"He gets very defensive."

"I thought it might help you get your mind off things. It's a story of hope and survival. Nothing at all like your story."

Death had a way of making small-talk seem even smaller.

"Your wife is right on that one. When you're invited to dinner, you take a bottle of wine as a token of your appreciation."

"At least they offered us a severance gift card."

"Rough meeting. Man, you really got hung out to dry."

"OK, let's start there. When did you first realize you weren't very compactible?"

"It's another squirrel – from the park. I warned you not to start feeding them."

"I was retaining water, so I cut out the salt. Now I retain gas."

"What? You're the one who sold me the universal remote control."

Stupid sink was still clogged. Now she'd either have to call a plumber or swallow what was left of the drain cleaner.

Next, I remember looking down at myself and thinking, Man, I don't look so hot. Maybe I should see a doctor.

"Exhibit A: the oxygen tube that came loose the night she died. You were there that night. You wanted to play then, too."

"I hope Mom and Dad get back together. I miss the hypocrisy."

"How long's he been out there?"

"Sorry, but we already know who we're going to hire for our new ethics director. We just posted the job for show."

GIVE ME HALF OF WHAT YOU STOLE AND I'LL LET YOU GO.

The old bad-cop, good-cop routine

"Worth as a person isn't tied to external validation. That said, as long as you can afford therapy, you're worth it."

"If you can't think of anything nice to say, how about a gift certificate?"

"With the handy remote you can adjust your exercise program from the couch."

"There were so many suspects who matched your description we ran out of room."

Bob kept missing the point and was forced to wait around for the next one.

"Inserting paper, lining it up, striking the keys, hitting the return carriage. I'd get him a computer, but he's doing just fine."

"Mind you, that's the worst-case scenario."

"It's a complicated case. I've advised my client not to say anything else until I speak to my lawyer."

"Took calcium supplements for years – without paying for them."

"And he said, Come unto me, for it's not what you know, but who you know."

"Put that down and have a seat. You can't take it into the session either. If I let you, I'd have to let everyone."

"Oh, I get it, you saw him first. So now *you're* the victim."

"Gee, duh, I don't know. Does it look like we have any in stock?"

The search for Big Foot continues.

"Let it go. Get on with your death."

"We find the defendant guiltyish."

Most cases of food poisoning can be avoided by being a little nicer to the waiter.

"They're getting awfully entitled."

FINANCIAL PLANNING

At least their adviser was good at explaining things.

"Hope you like the oversized furniture. It helps me feel young."

"It was a complete surprise when the table-setting police arrived. I had no idea I was doing it wrong."

"It's quite a learning experience. You'll be amazed at what you can live without."

"What can I tell you, we're short-staffed."

"Must be a computer glitch. It was supposed to go down in the third."

"I totally get the truth and justice thing, but what's with all the drama?"

Mothers want to help. They just can't help themselves.

Flat tire in the middle of nowhere. It was good to have a shoulder to cry on.

"Sure, it seems small. Anything would after driving around in a big old SUV."

"You were a shoo-in. Then I stumbled across your blog."

"Doctor-patient confidentiality doesn't extend to massage therapists."

"A little professionalism, people. When asking a patient to undress, we do not giggle."

"It's OK, everyone makes mistakes. Look at me. I hired you."

"Objection overruled. Answer the bloody question."

"And could you put in a louder horn?"

Always introduce the smallest guy first.

"It's not fair. I've got seniority."

"That's way too irregular. I recommend
regular exercise."

"You're just supposed to *watch*. They didn't ask for your advice."

"What about short-term? Where do you see yourself in five minutes?"

"We're holding our own, but I'd really like to see some growth."

"Don't worry about the past. Once you thaw out, try to chill-out."

"When on the stand, keep your answers short, to the point, and in the form of a question."

"And in local news: Bored housewife sells TV to buy crack."

"He said, 'I.' He'll say, 'do.' Just give him a moment to catch his breath."

"OK… and what about long-term goals?"

"The numbers don't look good.
Ironically, there's no quick fix."

"Wish you would've warned me about
this. I hate getting ambushed."

"Let's see if we can find one that's closer to people trying to sleep."

God finally admits there's a problem.

"We're having leftovers again. Don't worry, I shaved off all the fuzzy parts. I'm going to knit you a sweater."

Another childhood re-enactment hits a snag.

"Sorry I'm late. Couldn't find a parking space so I crashed into the building."

"OK, so, where were we? Oh right – I'm looking for someone to fill in for me while I'm in rehab."

The kind of help men go for.

Why the groom is never put in charge of anything.

"Our five-course dinners start with denial, followed by anger, bargaining, depression and finally acceptance."

"You could always ask to be home-schooled until it grows back."

"Just bring us whatever's scurrying around the kitchen floor."

"I need you to reassure the investors. Can you keep a straight face?"

"I can never tell with you. Are you trying not to laugh *at* me, or trying not to laugh *with* me?"

"It seems that you lack a sense of direction. I'll send you a better map."

"Tails it is. OK, that's how we'll take your temperature."

"He kept changing his will. In the end, it all went to legal fees."

"Maybe it's genetic. No one from her side of the family has shown up."

"That's better. The little scraper was giving me a hand cramp."

"You're a couch potato. These sessions are only making matters worse."

Doctors without Boundaries

Haystacks. The reason junkies hardly ever hang out in the country.

The proposal

"Always keep the upper hand – sup."

"Good boy. That's better than the others, but still too long. For playing fetch, I prefer a shorter stick, shaped like that, without bark or moss, and not quite as heavy."

"Very cool. What else can it do?"

"Of course I miss them, but what choice did I have? It was either them or me."

"I'm afraid of being left behind."

WATCH FOR POT HOLES

"This is excellent. Wow, it's amazing what we can accomplish when you let me take all the credit."

TIME TRAVEL AGENCY

"This coupon expired last week. Would you like to go back to redeem it?"

"However, I do hope to see a light at the end of the tunnel soon."

"It's not just a job. It's about being part of something bigger than yourself."

"That high chair is being recalled. Some kind of safety issue."

It wasn't going well.

"A few of us are getting together after work to binge-drink. You're welcome to join us if you're not in recovery."

"We had to close the change room. Too many people were just using it to put on puppet shows."

"I can too show gratitude. I'm just saving it for the right moment."

"Objection, deliberately misleading the witness."

"It's not a job; it's a calling. So, don't call us. It'll call you."

Build a bigger complaints box.

Dental records help ID the body. That's how they know who to bill.

"You won't find a better deal. Not for frameless."

"This is completely unacceptable. We're going to have to let you go."

"On the bright side, the dry heat really seems to be helping my arthritis."

It's not the destination, but the journey that counts. Until you screw up.
Then it's all about the destination.

"All in favor of just laughing it off, say
ha, ha, ha."

"It's a grueling job that requires a strong
commitment and personal sacrifice.
Is your mother available?"

"My first impression is that you have a false sense of entitlement. Now, get the hell out. I'm with another patient."

"You could've just thrown a pie, but no. You drove all the way home, in a tiny little car, just to get your gun."

Yes, there was the age difference, but somehow he always managed to push the right buttons.

"Relax, he's just doing his job. Try not to bite his head off."

"Mind you, I'm not responsible for the entire pipeline – just the section that flows through my office."

"Strange how times have changed. I used to hate spam."

"Every day I listen to your patients complain about the rat race. Well, my friend, I'm sick of the human race."

"Good point. It's been on the market far too long. I'll change the picture. I shouldn't be smiling."

"I came out to grab a larger size and got locked out of the change room."

"Mustard, ketchup and mayo are all nice and creamy smooth. Why isn't anything being done about relish?"

"They've rejected a number of offers. I guess they're in no hurry to sell."

"They kicked you out of the gifted class. You've been regifted."

"Thank you for calling the Coast Guard help line. To sink, press one. To swim, press two…"

Bob learned to redirect his pent-up fury. Rather than postal, he went coastal.

"Take it for stress. It helps to laugh at yourself."

"It's our first. Don't know where to begin. Haven't even picked out a domain name."

"I'm sick of holding out. If that's another buyout offer, I'm taking it."

Wasn't sure why, or even what it meant, but sometimes he just needed to make his presence felt.

"This one didn't turn out either. You must've moved."

"Our special tonight is buy two, get one free. Mind if I join you?"

"I was sure I'd gotten away with it. Optimism can add years to your life sentence."

"Wait until we reach the shore. You're portaging too soon."

"This is not what I asked for. I ordered a full-scale investigation."

"I began to think I was actually able to control the weather. The truth is, the weather was controlling me."

"Your problems are caused by all-or-nothing thinking. It's either that, or you don't have any problems."

"Car emissions are a major contributing factor to the glaciers melting. Our new designs take that into consideration."

"Can't be high-maintenance, but she must have class. Economy class."

"I'm under house arrest for six months. It's a lot more fun if you're not already in jail for a bunch of other crimes."

TRUE STORY

Each year strangers stop to pick mushrooms that grow at the front of our house.
They assure us they aren't poisonous – but never return.

"Never say, 'I can't do it.' Say, 'It may be possible.' Sounds less negative and more like the author of a self-help book."

"Steam from the boiler turns the turbine which then powers the air conditioner."

The carefully chosen Sorry-I-Can't-Pay-My-Gambling-Debt card helped soften the blow.

"Didn't think I even wanted one. I blame it on my biological cuckoo clock."

"It's simple, small and cheap. If she likes you, she'll probably like it."

"Under-the-bed monsters are pretty standard. We can remove it, but that'll void the lifetime warranty."

"They're born into captivity, it's all they know."

"I'm not finished exercising.
I still have a couple of laps to go."

Why cheap phones are a bad idea.

Unfortunately, napkins hadn't been
invented yet, so good ideas were
quickly forgotten.

The message was clear: Pay up or die.
Or maybe it was: Change the water.

"Three bedrooms, living room, dining room and plenty of room to negotiate."

"Call the plumber yourself. I'm swamped."

Lost in the shuffle, Bob refused to stop and ask for directions.

Even medical students sometimes
have to repeat a year.

Even while on vacation, Bob managed
to stand in the way of progress.

"The prefrontal cortex is involved in
higher mental functioning, like using a
can opener or remembering to feed you."

"Three bucks, and that's my final offer.
Three bucks to keep my mouth shut."

"Running away is serious business. Better pack another yogurt cup."

Employee Recognition Program

"Can Billy come out and compete in the global economy?"

"Six chipped teeth and a tongue stud infection. Good for you, no cavities."

"We managed to resuscitate him, but he's still very critical."

"We were only staying together for the kids. Now we're only staying together for the grandkids."

"Won the right to die without dignity."

"This batch tastes funny. Better boil it."

"'Litterbug' isn't politically correct. They prefer 'environmentally challenged.'"

"It's right here in the brochure:
'Be sure to tip your fishing guide.'"

"Nine years of college for this?"

"I'm Bob and this is my wife, Sue. Don't
even think about trying to get past us."

Once, I caught him with my passport, pasting his picture over mine. Bad dog.

"About the head-scarf: This is a place of business. Might want to tone it down."

"Relax. I was just messing with you."

Extreme Naturopathic Medicine.

"It's green, you colorblind, flea-bitten bonehead! Where'd you learn to drive?"

"Crazy bastard."

"I meant bring your fishing tackle."

"You're right, the numbers don't lie.
That's your job."

"The doctor will see you now."

"I'm anxious. Don't know why – I have a very comfortable lead."

"Quit interrupting me. You always did that when you were alive too."

"That easy chair used to be harder."

"Not sure when I'll be home – we're on another wild goose chase."

Second grade would prove to be much tougher than grade one.

"He's faking it. Must be feeling better."

"Gosh, I dunno. You sure it's organic?"

"Your husband suffers from delusions of grandeur. In fact, that's not even him in there – he hired a body double."

"I was found guilty and got three life sentences. Didn't know they could even do that."

"Why are you still here? I deleted you."

"It's simple, really – unless and until all our demands are met, we keep crying."

"Good, you're up. Feeling any better?"

God still told Bob what to do – but now the meds helped God be nicer.

Rule one: Never work without a net. Rule two: Be sure to specify the *type* of net.

"Care for anything else – an explanation perhaps?"

"Instead of trying to find the perfect cell mate, try being the perfect cell mate."

How cases end up in civil court.

"He's been having temper tantrums. Can you recommend a good anger management course?"

"Think of it as a legal loophole."

"You forgave her for that last week. When you forgive and forget you're not allowed to forget you forgave."

"Doctor says you've got to learn to relax – and not point a toy gun at police."

"It's a rags-to- riches story. You should take the company tour."

"We laid off too many people. Turns out, our only real revenue came from the employee parking lot."

"This is gobbledygook. I asked for mumbo-jumbo."

"I keep everything bottled up."

"I was just having fun. Get in touch with your inner-child – maybe she can explain it to you."

"You were talking in your sleep again."

"It's not a sale. It's a threat."

"Third one this month. Do you always have to analyze everything to death?"

"I was doing a lot of good, but then the funding ran out."

"I'm not late. Everyone learns at their own speed."

"Anything else you'd like to talk about, but can't – besides the vow of silence?"

"I had to report it. Based on your lifestyle, your heart attack was premeditated."

"He should be sensitive, but not overly sensitive – except to my needs."

"It's from his, 'Hey, my kid could do better than that' period."

"We may have to adjust the gastric band a little."

"The truth was, I had no one to blame but myself. And that's why I hired you."

"If you give up the right to remain silent, you get to keep all bragging rights."

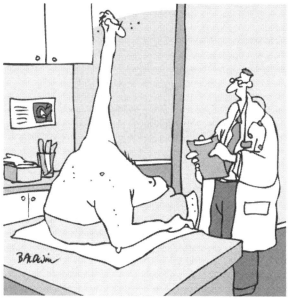

"You've got a buildup of creosote. It's no wonder: You smoked like a chimney."

"What, you mean like a bailout?"

"I've always been a bit of a ladies' man."

"I don't have time to explain. Just call the super and tell him the elevator's stuck."

"No, it isn't fair. Life isn't fair. If it was, everything would cost more."

"Just give him the money – but we'll need to hold onto the gun as collateral."

Money won't solve everything. Then again, neither will therapy.

"It's just a fairy tale. Try not to read so much into it."

"Let's not play hard to get. We both know it's a buyer's market."

"OK, now, drag him to the change room and find his wallet. Let's see if he has enough money to buy a new outfit."

"She says *I'm* the neighbor from hell?! Just tell her to keep her bloody dog quiet."

"And that pretty much sums it up."

"And in business news, it's now official: Everything *is* made in China. Citizens are encouraged to learn Mandarin, as well as how to march."

"It's called doctor-patient confidentiality. In layman's terms, you're paying me to keep my mouth shut."

"We've never had an accident – aside from two of our three kids."

"How worse? Give me the worst-case scenario."

"Of course they're small. What did you expect? They're floor *models*."

"She left everything to her cats."

"Forget the reward. It's too late to call Crime Stoppers. If you saw what happened, say so. "

"Heroin chic isn't the look I'm going for. Do you have anything more rehab?"

Getting him to open up was easy. He was pretty full of himself.

"Postpartum depression really hits you the day they turn 30, don't have a job and still live at home."

"Drop it. You're a watch dog. You're just here to watch."

"You need to start thinking outside the imaginary box."

"Human clinical trials start in six months. Sooner if we run out of mice."

"Sorry to interrupt, but this is our sixth session and that's your third notepad. When do I get to say something?"

"If you miss a payment, we will teach you a lesson."

"It's like caller ID. You get to see who's calling before you pick up."

"You don't really need a halo and wings. It's just a marketing gimmick."

"OK, you've been working like a dog. What's your point?"

"Cool, a wheel. Now you can take me shopping."

"Felt fine before I got here. Caught this from someone in the waiting room."

"If you have nothing to hide, why are you hiding?"

Talk to your plants – but never enter a suicide pact with one.

"Still stubborn as a mule."

"OK, but aside from putting on makeup, they can be used to keep an eye on the traffic around you."

Bob's lazy eye was getting worse – staying home, lying in bed and watching soaps all day.

SECURITY Dept.

KEEP
OUT

Innocent bystanders are real tough to convict.

"Do I know how fast I was going? Well, obviously, not fast enough."

"Sounds like a good deal. Would you be willing to take a polygraph test?"

"This next song is off my first album – before I souled out."

"Holidays are always the hardest – especially Christmas."

"He seems nice, but I wanted to hear all about your *project* mandate."

"How thoughtful. Thanks for the coffee."

"It's very rare. We don't even have a colored ribbon for it yet."

"Overruled. Now answer the question. We could all use a good laugh."

"Now's not a good time to split up. Perhaps once the economy improves."

"Heaven's great. It's just that now there's nothing to look forward to."

"Whoa! Aren't you a little big to be seeing Santa?"

"Oh, that reminds me. And the polar ice caps: I want them to stop melting."

Sistine Chapel – Extreme Makeover.

"I'm having difficulty dragging my butt out of bed each morning."

"I see the glass as half-full. Whereas he sees the glass and blames me for the naked man hiding in the closet."

"This next song is about setting boundaries, and how now I wish I had."

Next, I remember looking down and thinking, man, those pants make my butt look huge.

"If you have any other concerns, talk to the boss – his cave is always open."

"Keep your answers short. Long sentences lead to longer sentences."

"Wow, great marks. Don't tell Daddy – he already suspects you're not his."

"Kid's still awake. Hand me my taser."

Thanks to the air bagpipes, he walked away with only busted eardrums.

"Everything's designed for supermodels. What about supper models?"

"Once I learned where the problem was, I decided it would be best just to ride it out."

"Bought him a new pair of tap shoes. If he comes back to haunt me, I want to hear him coming."

"It's a good source of calcium and contains plenty of flabonoids."

"Can't believe I'm dating a guy who picks a fight at a salad bar – and loses."

"And make it look like an accident."

Gambling was in his blood. Couldn't help it – he had an irregular heartbeat. Even his pulse was impulsive.

Made in the USA
San Bernardino, CA
12 July 2016